Tongue Twisters to Teach Phonemic Awareness and Phonics

Beginning Blends and Digraphs
Grades 1-3

by Joyce Kohfeldt

Editors
Joey Bland
Tracy Soles
Tara Marini

Carson-Dellosa Art Adaptations
Bill Neville
Mike Duggins
Julie Webb

Dedication

To Jake Converse and Michael Gallagher, who make me want schools to be the best they can be.

ISBN 0-88724-582-X

Table of Contents

Introduction

Welcome to *Tongue Twisters to Teach Phonemic Awareness and Phonics: Beginning Blends and Digraphs*! The unique tongue twisters and engaging illustrations in this book are sure to bring many hours of enjoyment and instructional experiences to the students in your classroom.

> **The students in your classroom have literacy backgrounds that vary greatly. Some are:**
> - **Nonreaders who are listening to the sounds of letters in speech as their first experience with phonemic awareness**
> - **Nonreaders who are ready to use phonemic awareness skills to begin correlating sounds with letters in visual print (phonics)**
> - **Students who are ready to recognize the blends and digraphs in words**
> - **Students who can label elements in pictures and recognize the blends and digraphs in the words they say**
> - **Readers who can search for, recognize, and name many of the blends and digraphs in print**
> - **Students who will apply their phonics knowledge and create some tongue twisters of their own**

This resource provides something for each of these students and will appeal to:

☑ Readers who will enjoy hearing, repeating, and reading the tongue twisters just for fun

☑ Writers who will wish to create, and perhaps even illustrate, their own tongue twister sentences

☑ Students who will want to take copies of the tongue twister pages home to share the fun with their families

☑ Sleuths who will enjoy searching for Francis Frog, the frog hidden in each scene whose tongue gets tangled when he tries to say these tongue twisters

☑ Students who will want to revisit these tongue twisters again and again, either alone, in a small group, or with the whole class

Tongue Twisters to Teach Phonemic Awareness and Phonics: Beginning Blends and Digraphs is designed to be:

- **Flexible** so teachers select the order of activities and the formats to meet the needs of their students
- **Multi-level** so group lessons offer a range of opportunities to students ready for different levels of learning
- **Used with a variety of grouping patterns** so lessons could involve whole class instruction, small group instruction or reinforcement, individual work at the center, or as a take-home

Classroom Activities

While individual teaching styles and **the instructional needs of students will vary,** the following suggestions are start-up strategies for tongue twisters based on classroom experience and current research on phonemic awareness and the teaching of phonics.

- Have students **listen to and repeat each tongue twister** so they can hear and say the dominant sound.
- Have students **identify the tongue twister's beginning sound** through listening and repetition.
- Have students **name the blend or digraph that represents the dominant sound** they have heard and said.
- Have students **find the dominant blend or digraph in print** on each tongue twister page, either in the sentence or at the top of the page.
- Have students **initiate new words that begin with the dominant blend or digraph** of each tongue twister.
- Have students **search for and name items in each scene that begin with the blend or digraph**.
- Have students **search for and describe the location of the hidden Francis Frog**, who always gets his tongue twisted around words.

In addition to the 64 tongue twisters, this resource features a reproducible **parent letter** (page 9) to introduce the activities to the students' families. To help evaluate your students' progress, a **classroom observation guide** (page 11) has also been included. The guide will allow you to observe and assess your students' development in the areas of phonemic awareness and phonics, and then record their progress in a convenient chart. **Magnifying glass** patterns (page 12) to use in blend/digraph and picture searches and **award** patterns (page 13) to encourage and recognize your students' achievements are also included.

Teacher Preparation

The magnifying glass patterns can be used as visual tools in word and picture searches. After duplicating the patterns on card stock, cut out each shape. Then, cut out the center of each magnifying glass, and laminate them so they look like actual magnifying glasses. Now, the magnifying glasses can be used to search the tongue twister sentences, the blends and digraphs listed at the top of each page, and the illustrations.

Additionally, if you wish to create take-home books for your students, you will need to duplicate copies of the cover (page 10) and the tongue twister pages as you introduce them to your class.

Introducing the Tongue Twisters

Each Tongue Twister page has:

Some blends and digraphs listed at the top of the page and a magnifying glass to highlight the featured blend or digraph of that page

The tongue twister sentence with the featured blend or digraph that is bold and underlined at the beginning of words

The tongue twister scene with bolded images that match the words in the tongue twister, and between 1-4 extra unbolded objects that begin with the dominant blend or digraph of that page

Francis Frog who is hidden in each scene

Space for the student to draw another object that begins with the dominant blend or digraph of that page

Blair's mother Blanche bleaches blue blouses and black blazers.

You may wish to introduce one or two tongue twisters at a time with the same beginning blend or digraph. **The tongue twisters can be presented in any order, and can be sequenced to match the order of the sounds used in a basal program. Many teachers prefer to start with either a blend or digraph that begins the names of several students in the class. Their names help personalize the lessons for the students and provide extra motivation.**

> **Read the tongue twister several times to students, both at a regular rate and slowly. Ask them to listen for a blend or digraph they hear repeatedly. Have them repeat the tongue twister in its entirety. Or, if the tongue twister is long, students may repeat the sentence in segments as an echo after you have said it.**

It is important to note that some words in the sentences do not begin with the dominant blend or digraph. This format was deliberate. If every word in each sentence began with the dominant sound, there would be nothing for students to discriminate. It is important for students to listen to and recognize words that begin with sounds other than that tongue twister's dominant sound.

Introducing the Tongue Twisters

Listening to the tongue twisters will help students develop phonemic awareness as they repeatedly hear the same beginning sound in close proximity. As they listen for this sound, their brains become pattern detectors. Hearing and repeating the tongue twisters will help students to hear the sounds in speech and then reproduce them. These oral-mode experiences build the foundation for a student's ability to look at the tongue twisters and then recognize the same letters in print (phonics).

For older students, you may choose to have a child read the tongue twister aloud while the other members of the class listen and identify the dominant sound they hear. The students can list as many words as they can think of that begin with that sound. Then, they can self-correct their work by checking their lists against the tongue twister page.

Getting Started

Have the class look at the tongue twister page. Share with the class what blends and digraphs are. If two or more consonants appear together at the beginning of a word and you hear the sound of each letter, like in *bl* and *cr*, then the sound is called a *blend*. If two or more consonants appear together at the beginning of a word and the letters make one sound, like *sh* and *ph,* then the sound is called a *digraph.* If two or more consonants appear together in a word and you hear the sound of only one letter, like *kn* and *wr*, then the sound is called a *silent digraph*. **Point out that some blends or digraphs are printed at the top of each page. A magnifying glass highlights the featured blend or digraph.**

Then, **point to the tongue twister sentence at the bottom of the page, and call attention to the letters at the beginning of the words.** The letters of each word that begins with the dominant blend or digraph are bold and underlined. **This will support students who are just beginning to match and/or recognize the letters in print.** Students will now have distinguished and repeated the sounds (phonemic awareness) and connected the sounds to letters in print (phonics).

Classroom Detectives

One way to involve and motivate your students in these activities is to encourage them to become tongue twister sleuths. Using the magnifying glass pattern, demonstrate how they can scan the heading at the top of the page to find that tongue twister's featured blend or digraph. Students may also use the magnifying glass to scan the tongue twister sentence to find the words that begin with the dominant sound. On a more challenging level, students may wish to scan the sentence to find the featured blend or digraph anywhere in the words that make up the tongue twister.

In the center of each page is a scene that illustrates the elements included in the tongue twister. **Help your students develop visual literacy as you demonstrate how to explore the picture with the magnifying glass and search for the items mentioned in the sentence.** Scan the picture from the top left side of the page to the right. Using a return sweep to the left side, continue to scan the picture in a left-to-right motion until the picture has been completely scanned. This left-to-right movement and return sweep will help to reinforce the concepts of print and how to read: from left to right and from top to bottom.

As a support for emergent readers, the **objects featured in the tongue twister that begin with the dominant sound have been outlined with a heavier stroke in the scene (wherever possible).** You may point this out to students as they scan the illustration. Or, you may allow older students to discover this feature themselves, and tell you about that relationship.

Where is Francis Frog?

Have a student scan the picture with the magnifying glass to find Francis Frog. When the student describes his location, listen for and encourage the use of words like "beside," "in front of," "between," "to the left or right of," "inside," etc., that will help develop oral language.

Other students might be ready—either independently or with the entire class—to **scan the picture for other objects that begin with that tongue twister's dominant sound.** Each scene could have up to four additional items that highlight the dominant sound. An answer key of all the objects in each scene is included (pages 78-80).

After each tongue twister has been introduced, hang a copy of that page in the classroom, at the students' eye level. You may wish to have a student color the illustration before displaying it. You may also place a number beside each picture to indicate how many different tongue twister words can be found, either in the picture or in the sentence. Placing them at eye level will permit students to "read the room" and explore both the text and illustrations.

As an independent center activity, you may wish to duplicate the tongue twister pages so that students can color the items that begin with the dominant sound of each page. Additionally, there is space on each page for students to draw another object that begins with that tongue twister's dominant sound. If you choose to, your students may create a tongue twister take-home book. When a new tongue twister is introduced in class, students can add it to their collections at home.

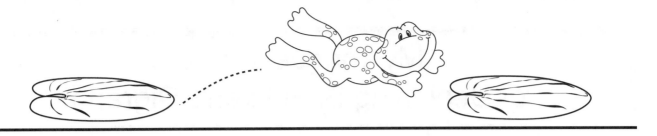

Dear Family,

My class is having fun learning about blends and digraphs like *ch*, *st*, *wh*, etc. We are:

- listening to and repeating tongue twisters where the same sound appears again and again
- finding objects in pictures that begin with that repeated sound
- looking for those blends and digraphs in words

You probably learned the tongue twister below when you were a child.

"Peter Piper picked a peck of pickled peppers. How many pecks of pickled peppers did Peter Piper pick?"

I will be bringing tongue twisters home so we can enjoy them together and create a book for our family. I bet your tongue will get twisted and tangled up, just like Francis Frog, when you say them!

If we do these together,

- I will learn the sounds that blends like *st* and digraphs like *wh* make.
- I will label the pictures and learn words that begin with different sounds.
- I will begin to recognize those blends and digraphs in words.

I am really excited about tongue twisters!

Love,

My Tongue Twisters
for Beginning Blends and Digraphs

sc   sh   sk   sl   sm   sn   sp   st   sw   th   tr   tw   wh   wr

Tricky Trixie tried to trade her trampoline for Trina's tropical tree house.

This Tongue Twister Book Belongs To:

_____

Tongue Twister Observation Guide for Blends and Digraphs

For Phonemic Awareness Monitoring and Phonics Knowledge

Observations may take place during whole class instruction or small group activities. You may use the following as a guide when assessing your students.

NY – not yet   **S** – some of the time   **M** – most of the time

A sample has been provided below for your reference.

Student's Name	repeats tongue twister	identifies blend/ digraph sound	names repeated blend or digraph	finds blend/ digraph in print	initiates words with same blend/ digraph	names other items in scene with same blend/digraph
Jason P.	9/12 M	9/12 S	9/30 NY	9/30 NY 10/15 S	9/30 NY 10/15 S	9/30 NY 10/15 S

Student's Name	repeats tongue twister	identifies blend/ digraph sound	names repeated blend or digraph	finds blend/ digraph in print	initiates words with same blend/ digraph	names other items in scene with same blend/digraph

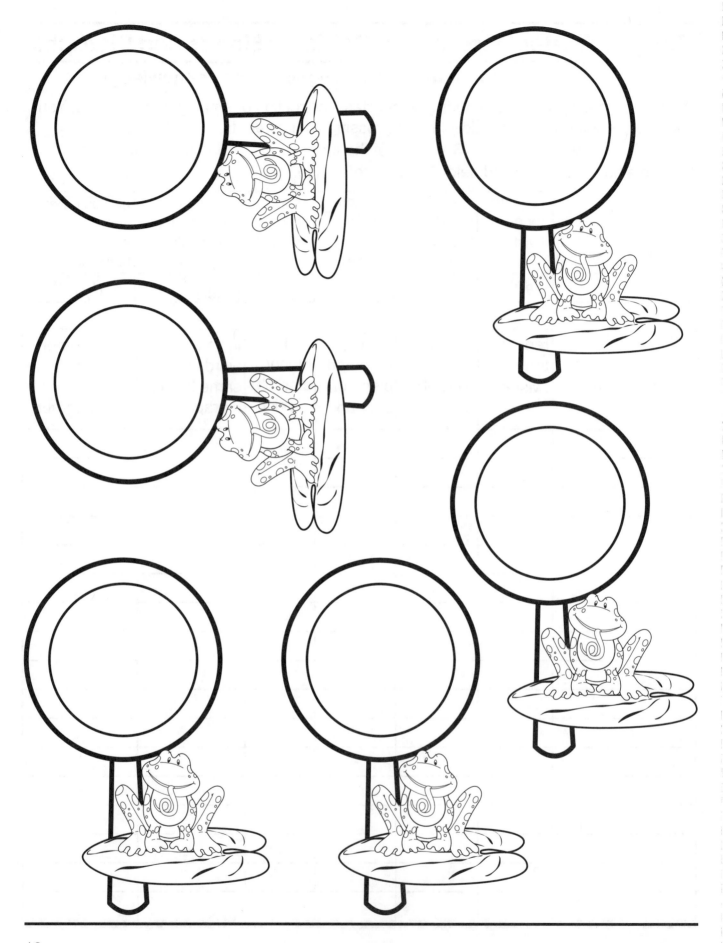

Reproducible

Francis Frog says,

"Well done, _____.

You are a tongue twister champ with blends and digraphs!"

_____
Signed

_____
Date

Francis Frog says,

"Well done, _____.

You are a champ at locating me in the tongue twister pictures!"

_____
Signed

_____
Date

Visit Blacksburg

Bleach

Blanche

Blueberries

Blair

Blair's mother Blanche bleaches blue blouses and black blazers.

Blimp

Go Big Blue!

Blake

Blossom

<u>Bl</u>ond <u>Bl</u>ossom wrapped herself in a <u>bl</u>ue <u>bl</u>anket on the <u>bl</u>eachers next to <u>Bl</u>ake.

bl (br) ch cl cr dr fl fr gl gr kn ph pl pr

Bruce's brother brought broccoli in brown boxes.

bl (br) ch cl cr dr fl fr gl gr kn ph pl pr

Brenda brings brown bran in a bright bowl to Brian for breakfast.

<u>Cl</u>eo <u>cl</u>eans <u>cl</u>othes out of her <u>cl</u>uttered <u>cl</u>oset.

On a c̲loudy day, C̲larence the c̲lever c̲lockmaker creates c̲lassy c̲locks out of c̲lay.

The <u>cr</u>awling <u>cr</u>ab <u>cr</u>ossed a <u>cr</u>ate of <u>cr</u>anberries.

The **cr**afty **cr**ocodile wore a **cr**own as he ate ice **cr**eam and **cr**ossed the **cr**ooked **cr**eek.

bl br ch cl cr (dr) fl fr gl gr kn ph pl pr

Drew dreamed of a funny, drowsy dragon in a dress.

bl   br   ch   cl   cr   (dr)   fl   fr   gl   gr   kn   ph   pl   pr

dragonfly

Drake

You Can Draw!

<u>Dr</u>ake <u>dr</u>opped and spilled the whole <u>dr</u>ink in the <u>dr</u>esser <u>dr</u>awer.

<u>Fl</u>o and <u>Fl</u>oyd <u>fl</u>ew to <u>Fl</u>orida to see <u>fl</u>amingos.

bl   br   ch   cl   cr   dr   (fl)   fr   gl   gr   kn   ph   pl   pr

F̲letcher waved a f̲lashy f̲lag to keep f̲lies away from the
f̲lowers.

25

<u>Fr</u>ances <u>fr</u>owned when <u>Fr</u>ank dropped her picture <u>fr</u>ame in <u>fr</u>ont of the <u>fr</u>idge.

bl   br   ch   cl   cr   dr   fl   fr   gl   gr   kn   ph   pl   pr

Fred's freckled friend likes french fries, fresh fruit, and
frankfurters.

Gloria Gleason wore gloves to glue gleaming glitter to a glass ball.

bl   br   ch   cl   cr   dr   fl   fr   gl   gr   kn   ph   pl   pr

Glenn gladly glanced at the glorious glacier.

Grace received a great grade for her graph of the Gray family grandchildren.

30

Grady the grocer helped Grandma and Grandpa Green with their groceries.

bl br ch cl cr dr fl fr gl gr kn ph (pl) pr

The Planets

First Place Gardener

platypus

Plato

Plato Platt places plenty of plants on a plastic platter.

The **pl**eased **pl**umber **pl**aces a **pl**unger and a pair of **pl**iers in **pl**ain sight.

bl   br   ch   cl   cr   dr   fl   fr   gl   gr   kn   ph   pl   pr

• Prague
Czech Republic

Aa Bb Cc

Prunes

Prince Preston promises to practice printing in private.

Happy Birthday **Priscilla!**

Prairie Dog

Prudy

$1.00

<u>Pr</u>incess <u>Pr</u>udy was <u>pr</u>oud of the <u>pr</u>etty <u>pr</u>esents she <u>pr</u>epared for <u>Pr</u>iscilla.

Happy Birthday!

Scarlet

Ice Cream

Are You Scared Yet?

to Scarlet from Scott

Scarlet received a <u>sc</u>out uniform, a <u>sc</u>ooter, and <u>sc</u>uba gear.

Corn

Scott

<u>Sc</u>ott the <u>sc</u>arecrow <u>sc</u>ares away the <u>sc</u>avenging crows with his super <u>sc</u>arf.

Skylar showed great <u>sk</u>ill on <u>sk</u>is, but her brother <u>Sk</u>ip liked his <u>sk</u>ateboard.

Sophia, the <u>sk</u>inny <u>sk</u>ater, happily <u>sk</u>etches <u>sk</u>unks on <u>sk</u>is and <u>sk</u>eletons.

Roxanne <u>sl</u>ips and <u>sl</u>ides on her <u>sl</u>ed down a <u>sl</u>ippery <u>sl</u>ope.

sloth

Sloane

<u>Sl</u>ender <u>Sl</u>oane ate <u>sl</u>ices of bread before <u>sl</u>owly <u>sl</u>ipping off to <u>sl</u>eep.

S̲m̲all children s̲m̲ile when they s̲m̲ear paint on their s̲m̲ocks.

sc   sh   sk   sl   (sm)   sn   sp   st   sw   th   tr   tw   wh   wr

Smitty smiled when he smelled the smoke from the campfire.

The <u>sn</u>ake <u>sn</u>oozed, then <u>sn</u>uck out when he <u>sn</u>iffed a <u>sn</u>ack.

sc sh sk sl sm (sn) sp st sw th tr tw wh wr

Maria **sn**aps a photo of the **sn**oring **sn**owman **sn**oozing in the

snow.

Spike's Restaurant in Spokane specializes in spicy Spanish rice and spearmint sponge cake.

Spencer spoils his cute spaniel Sparky with spaghetti, spareribs, and spinach.

The <u>st</u>ubborn <u>st</u>udent <u>st</u>opped at the <u>st</u>ationery <u>st</u>ore for <u>st</u>amps and got <u>st</u>uck in the <u>st</u>orm.

48

sc sh sk sl sm sn sp (st) sw th tr tw wh wr

Starlight's Stall

Welcome to Stinson's Stables

Stewart

_St_ewart _st_ands _st_ill and _st_udies the _st_allion in the _st_able.

Swedish Sweetheart
Swans

The **sw**ans **sw**ay and **sw**ish as they **sw**iftly **sw**im home.

The <u>Sw</u>ensons <u>sw</u>ap their <u>sw</u>eltering <u>sw</u>eaters for <u>sw</u>imsuits before

<u>sw</u>imming.

The Tripoli Express

Tracy

Trash

Tracy travels with tasty treats on her train trip to Tripoli.

<u>Tr</u>icky <u>Tr</u>ixie <u>tr</u>ied to <u>tr</u>ade her <u>tr</u>ampoline for <u>Tr</u>ina's <u>tr</u>opical <u>tr</u>ee house.

The __tw__ins __tw__isted __tw__ine around __tw__enty long __tw__igs at half past __tw__elve.

54

<u>Tw</u>ila felt sick after <u>tw</u>irling <u>tw</u>enty times and <u>tw</u>isting her toe

<u>tw</u>ice.

Schooner

Scholarship
Sign-up
Schedule

Sophie - 9:30

The <u>sch</u>oolteacher <u>sch</u>eduled a <u>sch</u>olarship interview for the <u>sch</u>oolgirl.

The man with the <u>scr</u>aggly beard ate <u>scr</u>ambled eggs and <u>scr</u>ibbled in a <u>scr</u>apbook.

402 Shreveport Lane

Carla

Shredded Lettuce Salad

Shredded Wheat

The Shrivers

Carla tossed the <u>shr</u>iveled <u>shr</u>imp and <u>shr</u>edded lettuce into the trash can beside the <u>shr</u>ubs.

58

A **spl**endid rain **spl**ashed and **spl**attered on the **spl**it rail fence.

The **spr**ay from the **spr**inkler **spr**ead water on the **spr**outs.

Juan **squ**atted down as he listened to the two **squ**abbling **squ**irrels **squ**eak.

The Great Strudel Struggle

Strange, striped fish stretched string across the stream in a straight line.

The **thr**ee kings were **thr**illed with **thr**ift shop **thr**ead as they sat on their **thr**ones.

Chelsea and Charles choose chili and chips.

bl br (ch) cl cr dr fl fr gl gr kn ph pl pr

Cheetah

Chandler likes chewing chocolate, cheese, chicken, and cherries.

The __kn__ight had a __kn__ack for __kn__eeling with a __kn__apsack full of __kn__itting.

bl br ch cl cr dr fl fr gl gr (kn) ph pl pr

Dave's **kn**obby **kn**ees **kn**ocked together when he wore **kn**ickers.

<u>Ph</u>oebe the **ph**otographer took a **ph**oto of a **ph**easant in <u>Ph</u>iladelphia.

bl br ch cl cr dr fl fr gl gr kn (ph) pl pr

Phillip the pharmacist phoned the pharmacy in Phoenix.

Shelby shares a shirt, shorts, and shoes with Shirley.

<u>Sh</u>ane <u>sh</u>ops for pretty <u>sh</u>ells, a <u>sh</u>ip, and a toy <u>sh</u>ark in a beach

<u>sh</u>op.

Thelma thanked Thane for taking the thorn out of her thumb.

Welcome to the Third Street **Theater**

Thirsty? Drink *Soda*

30 Thumbtacks

Thad

Thick'n Chewy Candy Bar

<u>Th</u>ad found a <u>th</u>ermos and <u>th</u>irty <u>th</u>umbtacks in the <u>th</u>eater.

Whitney's wheelbarrow held wheat bread, Whiskers, and a wheel.

sc   sh   sk   sl   sm   sn   sp   st   sw   th   tr   tw   (wh)   wr

Mr. Whitman
Dolphin Show
When: 3 p.m.
Where:
Dolphin Tank

Mr. <u>Wh</u>itman <u>wh</u>ispers to the <u>wh</u>ale <u>wh</u>ile he <u>wh</u>ittles.

The <u>Wr</u>ight sisters <u>wr</u>apped their <u>wr</u>eath in a paper <u>wr</u>apper so it wouldn't get <u>wr</u>inkled.

The <u>wr</u>iter <u>wr</u>ote about <u>wr</u>ecks and <u>wr</u>eckage on the sea floor.

Answer Key

Two-Letter Blends

Bl
Page 14
Blacksburg, blueberries, blocks, blender

Bl
Page 15
blimp, blowing leaves, Go Big Blue

Br
Page 16
Bradley Brothers Produce, bridge, brussels sprouts, broken foot, tree branch, bricks

Br
Page 17
briefcase, broom, brick wall, bracelet, braids

Bl
Page 18
clarinet, clipboard

Bl
Page 19
Clover's Clock Clinic, Cleveland, Sign up for Clock Class, clover

Cr
Page 20
crowbar, crane, cricket, crutch, Craig

Cr
Page 21
crow, crying, Crystal

Dr
Page 22
drink, drawer, drum, dresser

Dr
Page 23
You Can Draw, dragonfly, driveway

Fl
Page 24
Fly Fishing, flounder, flip-flops, flash

Fl
Page 25
flag pole, flashlight, flutter

Fr
Page 26
Freeze-O-Rama, Buy fresh vegetables Friday, fringe, Francis Frog, freezer

Fr
Page 27
France, Frozen Food, freezer, Francis Frog

Gl
Page 28
globe, Glenda, glass

Gl
Page 29
hang glider, gloves, glasses

Gr
Page 30
Grant, Greece, Gretchen Grover Elementary School, grass

Gr
Page 31
Granola, Grady's Grocery, Graham Crackers, grapefruit, grapes

Pl
Page 32
platypus, First Place Gardener plaque, The Planets, plate, placemat

Pl
Page 33
plane, plate, plaid shirt

Pr
Page 34
Prague, Prunes, pretzels, praying mantis

Pr
Page 35
Prairie Dog, price tag, propeller, slide projector

Sc
Page 36
ice cream scoop, scrap of paper, to Scarlett from Scott, Are You Scared Yet?

Sc
Page 37
scale, scoop, scowl

Sk
Page 38
ski lift, ski poles, ski boots, ski lodge

Sk
Page 39
ski poles, skates, Sketch Pad, ski goggles, ski pants

Sl
Page 40
Slater's Slippery Slope, Slow Ahead

Sl
Page 41
sloth, slippers, sleeping bag

Sm
Page 42
Sense of Smell, Mrs. Smart's Preschool, smoke detector

Sm
Page 43
Smith's Trail, Smoke Signals, Catching Small-mouth Bass

Sn
Page 44
snail, Ginger Snaps, sneakers

Sn
Page 45
snowmobile

Sp
Page 46
Spots In Space, Spike's Special Spinach Salad, spatula, spoon

Sp
Page 47
Spices, sports, Fresh Spinach, sponge, spoon

St
Page 48
Starfish Postcards, Stickers Buy One, Get One Free, Store Hours, Stewart's Stationery, steps, stool

St
Page 49
Welcome to Stinson's Stables, Starlight's Stall, stones, sticks, stepladder

Sw
Page 50
swing, sweeping, Swedish Sweetheart Swans

Sw
Page 51
Swiss Swim Team, Swanson Park Pool, swing set, swimming pool

Tr
Page 52
Trash, trumpet, trees

Tr
Page 53
tricycle, train, trophy, trees

Tw
Page 54
Twinkle, Twinkle The Life of Stars, Mark Twain, 20 yards

Tw
Page 55
Tweet Tweet, The Tweed Coat a play in 12 acts, twig

Three-Letter Blends
Sch
Page 56
Schooner, schoolbooks

Scr
Page 57
How to Write a Screenplay, screw, screen, Try our Scrumptious Scrambled Eggs

Shr
Page 58
Shredded Wheat, 402 Shreveport Lane, The Shrivers

Spl
Page 59
Spleet Tent Rental, Split Pea Soup

Spr
Page 60
Spring Flowers, Spruce, Fairies and Sprites

Squ
Page 61
Fresh Squeezed Juices, Summer Squash

Str
Page 62
The Great Strudel Struggle, strawberries

Thr
Page 63
The Singing Thrush, Threshold Castle

Digraphs
Ch
Page 64
chives, cheese, Chapter 3, chalk, chalkboard

Ch
Page 65
Chastity, chores, Cheetah, chair, checkered shirt, chewing gum, checks

Kn
Page 66
knots, knife, knee

Kn
Page 67
Knickerbocker Knockwurst Sandwiches, The Knack of Knockout Golf

Ph
Page 68
Philadelphia Philharmonic Concert, I ♥ Phonics, phone, phone booth

Ph
Page 69
Photo Developing, Phoenix Postcards, Phyllis, Phoenix Phone Directory

Sh
Page 70
shelf, ship, shampoo

Sh
Page 71
Shark Teeth 10¢ each, Explore the Shore, shovel, shorts, shoes, shelves

Th
Page 72
thimble, thermometer, Thanksgiving Day Sale

Th
Page 73
Thirsty? Drink Soda, Welcome to the Third Street Theater, Thick 'n Chewy Candy Bar

Wh
Page 74
White House, whistle

Wh
Page 75
When: 3 p.m., Where: Dolphin Tank, wheelchair, wheels

Wr
Page 76
Write-a-Wrapper, wrench, writing

Wr
Page 77
Bill Wrigley, candy wrapper, Wright's Wreckage Inc.